# Heart Prayers

## Poems, Prayer, & Meditations

# Heart Prayers
Poems, Prayers, & Meditations

*Peggy Haymes*

PEAKE ROAD

Macon, Georgia

ISBN 1-57312-098-7

*Heart Prayers*
*Poems, Prayers, & Meditations*

Peggy Haymes

Copyright © 1997

Peake Road
6316 Peake Road
Macon, Georgia 31210-3960
1-800-747-3016

*Library of Congress Cataloging-in-Publication*

Haymes, Peggy
    Heart prayers: poems, prayers, & meditations/Peggy Haymes.
    vi + 90 pp.                    5.25" x 7.75" (13 x 19 cm)
    ISBN 1-57312-097-9 (alk. paper)
    1. Prayers. I. Title.
    BV245.H36        1997
    242.8—dc21                              96-40444
                                                CIP

# Contents

# *Introduction*

Dear God,
Here I am
    with a heart full of words
    that choke and stumble
    and get in each other's ways.
Here I am
    with a soul longing
    to bathe in your waters,
    yet a soul terrified
    of your touch.
Here I am
    knowing that you are
    my only true home,
    yet lingering on the front porch
    not quite sure
        that I belong.
I have known you forever.
And not at all.
So hear my stumbling,
        stuttering
        prayers of longing
            and hope
            and fear
            and gladness
            and love.

# *Places Along the Way*

Maybe it was the "late in life" travel plans of Abraham and Sarah. Maybe it was the "forty years 'til we get there" trip of the children of Israel from Egypt to the Promised Land. Maybe it's because the earliest followers of Christ were called people of the Way. Or maybe it's just because there is so much truth in the image.

For whatever the reason, we return over and over again to the image of the life of faith as a journey. Like any good trip, it is a journey of high, holy times and of everyday routine. But if we have willing eyes and faithful hearts, we may see something of God in all of it.

# *I Want to Be the Woman*

He taught himself Greek
    at eighty years old
    because he'd always wanted to learn.

God,
I want to be like that!

I want to be the woman
    taking the course
    with the half-century head start
      on her classmates.

I want to be the woman
    who cherishes the secret
    she's discovered
    that once you're old enough
      you can get away with
      wearing tennis shoes
      anywhere
        and with anything.

I want to be the woman
    who's always hopeful enough
    to plant another batch of bulbs
    in the fall.

I want to be the woman
    who always finds herself among teachers,
    some of whom are children
      and teenagers.

I want to be the woman
    who knows
    that there's always
        some new place to discover
        up the road,
        across the ocean,
        in my heart.

I want to be the woman
    who, for her 106th birthday
    wanted to go dancing—
        and did.

God,
Surely such people make you smile.
    I want to be like that.

# *Blackout*

The lights just went out,
    and here I am with
    a morning of writing to be done.
The room where I have nested myself
    is now dark and full of shadows.
        And I have writing to do.

So I do what I can,
    picking myself up,
    moving into another room
    where the morning light
        wanders in through eastern windows.

What a simple, ordinary lesson, God,
    for those days when it seems
        as if the lights have gone out,
    for those days when it seems
        as if all is dark.
            Perhaps all I can do in that moment,
            perhaps the most I can do in that moment,
            perhaps the best I can do in that moment
                is move to another room
                where there is more light.
Some days, God, it may not be much of a move
    and there may not be much light for me to find,
        and maybe some days
        the most I can reach for
        is the promise of light restored.
            But give me the courage
            to reach nonetheless.

# Kairos

I'd been knocking on the door for months
    when suddenly,
      when I least expected it,
        it opens.
My mind had been fumbling in frustration
    with the problem
    with no good answer in sight
      when suddenly something clicks,
      a piece falls into place,
        and the way is clear.
The pages of the book
    had been disappointingly lifeless to me
    until that day when I pick it up
    and it bursts into flames
      (metaphorically, of course)
        and I can't turn the pages
        fast enough.

Kairos time.
At the right time.
    Just the right time.
    The moment when the bud
      decides to open into flower.

God,
    we are so silly sometimes,
    armed with our appointment books
      with neatly lined blocks of time,
      our watches and stopwatches—
        as if we controlled all of our time.

But Kairos comes and goes like the wind.
We cannot force the moment.
　　　So at least let me look up from my schedule
　　　　　long enough
　　　　　　　often enough
　　　　　　　　　to welcome it.
　　　　　　　　　Kairos.

# Being Still

The bags are unpacked,
    the groceries put away,
    and finally I am alone,
        finally I can be still.

I fled to the mountains like a refuge.
I came to this cabin
    to escape the distractions
        of telephone
        and laundry to be done,
        and everyday places to go.
I came seeking silence,
        solitude,
        stillness.

I'd dreamed of it,
looked forward to it,
kept a smile on my face thinking about it.
    So why is it so hard?

I want to jump up
    and find a million things to do,
    run another errand,
    take on another task.

God, what is it
    I'm afraid I'll hear
        by being silent?
What is it
    I'm afraid I'll find
    by being still?

# *Fear*

Slowly it spreads,
    cold fingers reaching
    until my heart is encased
    in the hard ice of fear.

So cold,
I cannot feel the warmth
    and the caring
        offered to me,
        offered all around me.

So thick,
it stops the light of my shining soul
    and holds it back,
    holds it in
        until even I believe
        there is no light at all.

So hard,
it freezes me,
paralyzes me
    until I cannot move,
        I cannot speak.

Slowly it spreads
    until I can only pull into myself,
    wrap my arms around myself
        to stave off shivers,
        no way left to embrace,
            to reach,
            to give.

"Fear not."
Did you get tired of having to say it, God?
"Don't be afraid . . ."
Did you ever grow weary
    of having to remind them
    over and over again?

Please, God,
    once again,
    remind me.

Please God,
    with the light of your love,
    warm the cold around my heart.
With the light of your love,
    melt away my crystal prison,
    catching the water-tears
        that flow with hope
        and with trust.

"Don't be so scared . . ."
Dear God,
    say it to me again,
    remind me again,
        over and over again
        until my heart hears.

# Perfect Moments

For that one moment, God, everything was perfect.
It was the savoring of food and conversation
     while a fresh snow fell out the window.
It was the music
     that sang to the best places
     in my soul and in my day.
It was the gentle morning on the beach
     with the air and the breeze and the ocean
     all in perfect harmony.
It was a drive through the country
     on a sunny Saturday morning
          or the rain on the roof
          as I drift off to sleep.
It was receiving just the right card
     from just the right person
     at just the right moment.

Sometimes, God, we say
     that nothing in life is perfect.
But we're wrong.
Just every so often
     that moment comes,
     and hopefully I am alive enough,
     and aware enough
          to know . . .
               For this moment,
               everything is perfect.

# Tears

Finally, the tears come,
 tears flowing clear across my soul,
 washing away
 the heavy weight
 of loss ungrieved,
  unmourned,
  unnamed.
Finally, the tears come
 bringing release and relief.
  No wonder it's called
  a good cry.

So why are we so ashamed of our tears, God?
Why do we brush them away,
  brush them off,
 apologize for them
  as if we've done something wrong?

How could we forget the sight . . .
 you weeping by the grave of a friend,
 you weeping for a city so blind
  it could not see love standing at its gates,
 you weeping for yourself
  because you were human
  and you did not want to hurt
     and suffer
     and die.
How could we forget
 that in the gift of our tears
 flows the healing water of grace?

# For Now

For now, God,
    just let me sit.

For now,
    let questions be quiet,
    let fears fade,
    even let my concerns
        for family and friends
        and families of friends
        slip to the sidelines.

For now, God,
    for this one moment,
    just let me sit with you
        in the way of friends
        who can tell each other everything
        but can sit together without saying anything.

Let me sit
    with the love that has cradled me,
        the strength that has sustained me,
        the peace that has wrapped me in its warmth,
        the grace that has picked me up
            and put me back on my feet again.

Let me leave behind my laundry list
    of choices to make,
    things to do,
    wants and wishes and dreams.

For this moment, God,
    let me seek
    only you.

# My Never-Broom

Today, God,
    as I was sitting with my dreams,
    I began shooing them away
        like unwanted children.
            Get out of here.
            You don't belong.
            You'll never be able to stay,
                so why should you visit?

Never.
That's the word
    I kept singing like a refrain.
        Never.
        Never ever.
        Why encourage those dreams
            when they come around?
            Because they will never move in
                    and live with me,
                never be transformed
            from hope to reality.

And then I look around.
I see so much
    that is so matter of fact
    a part of my life,
        familiar and mostly taken for granted.

And with a start
    I realize
    that this, too, had once been
    only a dream—

dreams that I tried to shoo
out of the house
using my Never-broom.
It will never happen.
I'll never have/do/be.
Never.
Once I tried to sweep these children
out of my life
with my Never-broom,
but they kept coming back,
claiming a room,
moving in,
becoming mine,
becoming real.
(Although
I have to admit
that some of them have grown up
to look quite different
than I ever imagined they would!)

God,
some of these dreams
I'm not so sure about.
But help me lay my Never-broom aside,
at least to give them a chance,
at least half a chance.
And who knows?
Maybe some of them will decide to stay.

# Control

Do you ever get tired, Lord,
  of me telling you what to do?
    I need to go here.
    I need to do this.
It's as if I don't trust
  that you can figure it out on your own.
So like giving directions to a child,
  I spell it out.
    Open this door.
    Open it this way.
    Open it now.

Forgive me, Lord,
  for assuming that I need to control
  all things in my life . . .
    even you.
Especially you.

Grant me the grace
  to share with you
  my dreams
  and hopes
  and fears . . .
    and to trust you with the rest of it.
Help me to trust
  that you will indeed lead me
  in a way that leads to life.
Let me tell you what I desire,
  the good and bad and selfish and noble,
  then trust you to sift through,
    to hold gently,
    to do with me as you will.
      And that will be prayer enough.

# Your Promises, Lord

Your promises, Lord,
> sometimes they are as clear to me
> as morning's first light
>> dazzling and daring in the ice-covered
>> branches.

The clarity,
> the sureness of it all
> makes me want to catch my breath,
>> to dance for joy,
>> to shiver with delight.

But sometimes, O Lord, the promises sound worn,
> gray like the snow that's stayed too long.
>> Just cold.
>> Just empty.

I've heard the same words for so long,
> and God, forgive me,
> it seems as if I've been hoping the same hope
>> for too long.

And I must cry with the psalmist,
> How long, O Lord?

Like Abraham and Sarah, Lord,
> teach me hope for the long road,
> teach me hope for the days yet delayed.

Like Abraham and Sarah, Lord,
> forgive me when I give up
> and give out.

Keep taking me by the hand
> until I am in the land
> of your promise.

From *Reflections* (Macon GA: Smyth & Helwys, January–April 1995). Used by permission.

# Speaking

What if . . .
    What if I spoke and no one heard?
What if . . .
    I spoke and no one was listening,
    or no one paid attention,
    or everyone laughed at me?

Speaking out loud is scary stuff.
And it's much easier
    if I use someone else's voice.
        A voice with authority
            like teachers
            or leaders.
        A familiar voice
            like family
            or friends.
                That would be safe, you know.

God, what if I speak
    and no one understands?
What if I speak
    with the language of my heart
    and I am left to stand alone?
What if I speak
    with the words of my heart
            and my mind
            and my soul
            and they see
                    Me?

God,
Are you sure
    you mean
    for me to use
    my own voice?

# *Wrong Side of the Bed*

God,
I'm not so sure
you want to hear my prayers this morning.
I awoke
    already out of sorts,
    with eyes ready to spot a slight,
    with ears that seemed perpetually out of tune.

So what should I do
    with such a morning?

I can wrap my ill-will around me
    like a fierce blanket.
I can use it like a flyswatter,
    swatting away anyone who dares to come close.
I can put it away,
    shut it in a closet,
    dress myself in a smile
    and convince my friends
        that I greeted the day
        with a bluebird on my shoulder.

Or . . .
I can stop to listen to out-of-sorts cries,
    to sort through them myself,
    to let go what is too old and silly and small to hold,
    to hear as well the strangely twisted signal
    that something is out of kilter in me,
    something that matters,
    something that needs tending.

God,
    what shall I do with such a morning?

# How Can It Be, Lord?

How can it be, Lord,
    that I love you so deeply
    and yet am so careless with that love?
How can it be
    that in a moment I know
        my need for you,
        just as surely as I need the air I breathe.
But when that moment is past,
    I return
    to letting everything
    and everyone come before you.
In one breath, I declare my love,
    and in the next declare
    that there is no time to spend with you.

Tomorrow . . .
Next week . . .
When I have time . . .
        Don't you see the work that waits on me?
        Don't you see my long list of things I have to
            do?
        Don't you understand?

Sometimes I wonder, Lord,
    which grieves your soul more,
        those who deny you,
        those who oppose you,
            or those who are simply indifferent,
            working you in when time permits.

# Prove Me
## (Psalm 26)

God,
I'm afraid that the psalmist
    is just a little more confident than I am.
"Prove me," he says.
"Test my heart and mind."

Me,
I usually take a different approach.
I welcome you into the house of my soul
    and say,
        "Could you not look so closely?
        There's a lot
            I swept under the carpet
            that I'd rather you not see."

The psalmist says,
    "Test me,"
    and I usually say,
    "Ummm . . . do you have an easier route?
    Point me to the bunny slope of life."

The psalmist says,
    "My foot is no level ground,"
    while I keep tripping over my own shadow.
But maybe we aren't so far apart,
    he and I,
    because in the end
        in confidence or confusion,
        we still come around to the same place.

You.
Your love.
        Your grace.
        The blessing of the best in us
        and the hope of all the rest.

Prayers of faith
        and of fear,
        you hear them all.

"For your steadfast love
        is before my eyes,
        and I walk
        (or at least stumble)
        in faithfulness to you."
                Amen and amen.

From *Reflections* (Macon Ga: Smyth & Helwys, May–August 1996). Used by permission.

# *Loving Self and Neighbor*

Why is it, Lord,
   that I find it so easy
   to attend to everyone else's spiritual growth,
   but neglect my own?

Why is it a good thing
   when I encourage them
   to reflect and read and meditate and pray,
   but when I take such time for myself,
I feel vaguely guilty.
   Shouldn't I be doing something?
   Shouldn't I be doing for someone else?

In my best moments, Lord,
   I know that it's not selfishness
            that calls me forth
            to times of silence
            and solitude
            and reflection,
               but rather your liberating voice.

For in such moments
   I clear away the brush that blocks my way.
In such times
   I face the fears that keep my heart
            from brave and bold dreams.
   I loosen the chains of doubt
            that too long have held my spirit.
   I discover old wounds too long festering
            and bring them into the light of your healing
               grace.

From such times,
>    I turn with stronger hands for helping,
>    clearer vision for serving,
>    lighter heart for singing . . .
>>        and freed feet for dancing.

Love your neighbor as yourself.
That's the way you put it.
>    Remind me
>    that you didn't mean it to be one or the other,
>    either/or.
>>        Love them.
>>        Or love myself.

Remind me
>    that you created our hearts
>    big enough for both.

From *Reflections* (Macon GA: Smyth & Helwys, September–December 1996). Used by permission.

# Interruptions

God,
I don't have time for this.
    I have a full calendar.
    I have people depending on me.
    I have things to do.
        I don't have time
        for such interruptions.

The little interruptions . . .
The survey-taker's phone call
    in the middle of fixing dinner.
The button that comes off the shirt
    or the run that springs in the brand new pair of
        hose.
The lawn mower that won't start.

Bigger interruptions . . .
the car that breaks down,
the cold that slows me down,
the phone call that must be tended to right away.
        The unexpected detour along the journey.
        God, I don't have time for this.
        Surely you know
            this isn't what I had planned.
I don't like the disruption of it,
    the frustration of it,
    the helplessness of it.
        I don't like the interruption.

But I don't think they're going away.

Like a good sailor, God,
    help me navigate my course,
    not only when the breeze is steady,
    but also when the wind
        freshens and falls and suddenly shifts.

Forgive me
    the presumption and arrogance
    of believing
        that everything
        should always go
            as I've planned.

And perhaps, God,
    give me an extra measure of grace
    to see you in the spaces
    interruptions create
        in my days.

# For a Moment, Lord, I Felt It

For a moment, Lord, I felt it.
A refugee from the days
    when rainbows still delighted my eyes
    and all of life was a passion.
Somehow untouched
    by grown-up voices of practicality
    and cynical voices of dire predictions.
I felt the chill bumps
    and the light shining from my eyes
    as I danced on the edge of dreams and visions.
Dreams of being more
    than what I have become.
Visions of holy passion
    that set fire to my days.

Dreams and visions
    that light up a gray world
    with technicolor hope.
        But of course, I could never . . .
        But of course, it would never work . . .

Could it be, Lord?
Could it be
    that in these things
    I want to so casually write off
        as childishness
        and foolish nonsense,
Could it be that you are there
Somewhere?

# I Wanted Water

I wanted a glass of water, God.
Everything in me said
        that what I needed
        was a glass
                of cold,
                clear,
                simple water.

So why did I reach
        for a soft drink instead?

Why, God,
        do I do that?
        I know what my heart wants,
        what my spirit is longing for,
        what my soul needs.
And still I reach
        for the cheap imitation,
        empty of that which I need,
        full of that which I don't need.
                Because it has the fancy commercials,
                the cool reputations . . .
                        the real one,
                        the choice of the young,
                        those in the know.
So full of promises
        that go flat so quickly.

God,
>     why do I spend so much time seeking my heart
>     only to ignore it?
> Why do I spend my time and energy
>     seeking your wish for my life
>     only to turn away from it?

God,
>     when my soul is so thirsty,
>     why do I turn away
>         from your cool waters?

God,
>     help me listen
>     to the wisdom of my heart.
>         Help me to reach
>         for that which I need
>         instead of what I've been told to want.

# I Expect So Much of Myself, Lord

I expect so much of myself, Lord,
    and so little.
Somewhere deep inside
    hides the hard demand
    that I be equal to any challenge,
    that I never fail or falter,
    that I get it right.
That I always get it right.

God, forgive me
    for worshiping at perfection's altar.
God, forgive my arrogance
    that assumes
    that if I only try hard enough
        and work hard enough
I will never, ever need grace.

I ask too much of myself, Lord,
    yet I sell myself short,
    for too quickly I forget
    that I am a beloved child of God.
        Created.
        Loved.
        Embraced.
        Gifted.
        And known.
Forgive me, Lord,
    and remind me
    that you have already

set a place for me at the table,
invited me to come.

I don't have to earn my right,
I don't have to work my way in,
I don't have to sneak through the back door
lest you discover I really don't belong.

I am your child,
And that is enough.
That is more than enough.

# I Was Angry Last Night

I was angry last night, Lord,
    jaw-clenching,
    fire-breathing,
    smoke-spitting angry.
Now I find that the fresh morning air
    has cooled some of the heat
    that set my blood boiling.
I was angry last night, Lord
    and the truth of it is
    that I don't want to let go of it.
At least, not all of it.

I want to let go
    of the cruel, corrosive acid
    that eats away at my soul.
        But I don't want to let go
        of its power and its strength.
For I breathe a little deeper,
    and feel a little stronger,
    and touch again
        that rock-hard place of determination
        that wrong shall not have the last word,
            that what ought not to be shall be no more.
Teach me, O Lord,
    how to be angry,
    lest I confuse
        a bruised ego
            with a broken creation,
        an imagined slight
            with all too real injustice,

and inconvenience
with hurdles and mountains
and locked gates
shut by hatred's hand.
Teach me, Lord,
how to hold on to what should not be forgotten,
how to let go of what need not be remembered,
how to be angry . . .
and sin not.

# Sometimes, Lord, I Get Impatient

Sometimes, Lord,
> I get impatient.
I know you have promised to provide for today,
> but it's tomorrow
> and the day after,
> and the year after
>> that I'm worried about.

The children of Israel wandered
> for forty years,
> and sometimes I wonder
> if we don't have the same travel agent.
I don't want to be guided
> by the fire and by the cloud,
> step by step.
I want long-range plans
> detailed road maps
> with detours few and far between.

Yet when I stop
> and remember the road behind me,
> it is a wonderment . . .
The sure dead ends turned into new beginnings,
Roads I would not have chosen
> that have led me through places of grace.
The unexpected views along the detours
> whose beauty rolled over me
> like a gently breaking surf.

Be patient with me, Lord,
for sometimes my trust
is as fragile as a china teacup,
and sometimes my faith
is that small.

Be patient with me,
forgive me for whining
like a small child on a long trip.
Guide me,
and direct my steps
for all of the hours of this day . . .
and the rest will come.

# I'm Tired, Lord

I'm tired, Lord.
I'm tired of the same problems,
   the same questions
That keep making their way
Back to my soul
  like homing pigeons.
I'm tired of running the same track
  over and over
  and over again.
I'm tired of whirlwind days,
  and crowded calendars,
  and squeezed-in schedules.

I'm tired, Lord.
 Just tired.
   My body cries out,
   my mind cries out,
   my soul cries out
     for rest.

And yet I act as if
  I can bring your kingdom in
  with sheer breathlessness.
I act as if
  the world will stop turning
  if I am not there
  to supervise the rotations.

Lord, you promised us rest,
  yet I can't seem to slow down enough
  even to receive
  the gift I crave.

Could you help me, Lord?
Could you help me give up
    my devotion to endless running?

Could you help me
    to trust you enough
    to stop for a minute,
    to let myself go,
    to let the world go,
To float lightly on the soft,
    sweet,
        gentle streams of your peace?
            For I'm tired, Lord.

# *Creating*

The hours swept by
    as careless as seconds
    as I lost myself in my work.
Music filled the spaces of my home
    as painting filled my attention,
        my world as small as the canvas before me,
        as big as the universe.
How does that line flow?
How do I capture that color,
        that texture?
            Not quite.
            Not quite.
            Not quite.
                Yes.

I look up and find
    an entire evening has passed,
    and I'm as relaxed
        as an old cat in the sun.

But when the paining's done,
    I grow rigid with a critic's pose.
        This isn't any good.
        This isn't as good as someone else would do.
        Why did I think I could paint?

God,
    the great Creator,
    teach me your lessons.

Give me the grace and the wisdom
        to call my work good
        not because it would win a show
            (for it wouldn't)
        or measure up to someone else's standard's
            (which it might not),
                but simply because
                its creation
                brought me joy and delight.
Simply because
        for those magical hours
        I lost myself . . .
            I found myself.


Teach me, God,
        to celebrate the gift of creating.
                    And behold,
                    it was very good.

# Traveling Companions

As much as we'd like to see ourselves as heroic and solitary individuals setting off to face foreign lands alone, the truth of it is that we always have an abundance of traveling companions. Some of them we'd choose, such as a long-awaited trip with old friends. Some are strangers bearing unexpected gifts. Some of them bring to us questions that disturb us and unsettle us, and perhaps that is gift as well.

# Hammering Down

Hammering down . . .
The bluegrass players know it well,
    hammering down a guitar string
    to change the note
        that's being played.

Hammering down . . .
I hammer down shingles
    on a hot summer roof,
    hoping,
    praying
        that the house taking shape
    beneath my feet
        will change the notes
        of a family's life.

What kind of song, God,
    can you sing from a shack
    when the cold comes in
        or the rains drip through
        and uninvited critters have their run of the
            place?

What kind of music is it, God,
    for a kid who's too embarrassed
    to bring a friend home to play?
What kind of music is it, God,
    when rough walls puncture any dreams
    before they get a good start?

Hammering down . . .
Dear God,
    may my clumsy carpentry
    be an offer of new music
        for this family and this world.

# Waiting Rooms

I know
    there are grander cathedrals on this earth,
    but there are no
        holier places than this.
God, it's like watching grace
    being spun before your eyes.

They are all so different,
    the wealthy and the poor,
    black and white,
    large families and people by themselves.
They are all so much alike,
    waiting through the hours
        for the few precious moments of visit,
    waiting for the doctor
        to give the latest word,
    waiting,
    hoping not to wait for the news
    that begins,
        "I'm sorry . . ."

They sleep in their chairs
    and in their clothes
    for days and nights and nights and days on end.
They share each other's food
    and take each other's phone calls.
        And when the bad news comes,
        even in the dark stretches of morning,
        they wait with one another.

God,
I know it's fashionable to say
    there's no community anymore,
    that we don't know each other,
    that we don't care about each other,
    that we are all strangers.
        But these folks don't know that yet.
        Camped out in a waiting room
        'round the corner from intensive care,
            they find each other . . .
                and holy ground.

# Retreat

We haven't the time to get away.
You know that, God.
    Our weekends are full
        of houses to be cleaned
        and yards to be tended
        and a thousand things to be done
            that we have no time for during the week.

It's too much trouble to get away.
You know that, God,
    for there are schedules that must be juggled,
    arrangements to be made,
    clothes to be packed.

Yet somehow we've done it.
We gather in a cabin warmed by the fire
    and the smell of cinnamon-rich cider
        simmering on the stove.
One by one,
    we take off all of the hats we wear,
    employee, spouse, parent,
        until we are left with ourselves.
We wear comfortable clothes
    and let our souls relax.
        And we talk together of everything and nothing.
        We share silly jokes and sacred stories.
        We eat often and with delight,
        and go to bed far later,
            or earlier,
            than usual.

We wander around in your stories
    and sit with you in prayer,
        for once not distracted and tugged on
        by all that must be done.

People we've known for years
    we suddenly discover as friends.

We haven't the time
    to go away this weekend, God.
    you know all we have to do.

But you know all that we need.
So keep reaching through
    all our excuses
    to call us away
        to a deserted place.

# *She Was Dying*

She was dying, God.
She knew it.
    We knew it,
    although I could only imagine
    the constant companion
        of her pain.

She was dying,
    and yet chose to spend
    the final,
        precious,
        measured months
        working.

Working on her life.
    Finding old hurts
        locked away by fear
        now claimed and healed
            by the light.
    Finishing neglected matters
            too long left
            unfinished.

Choosing to be
    completely alive
    in the face of her death.
        God, what courage she had.

So often we take our lives for granted,
    letting the days slip through our fingers
    like a careless child
    holding too many toys.

We go along, get along,
    are swept along
        by whichever voice
        shouts the loudest.
We throw the hours away
    as if there'll always be more.

But she was dying.
She knew it.
    We knew it.
    And she chose to live.

God, thank you for women and men
    of courage and of hope.
Thank you for the ones
    who show me how to be alive.

God,
    give me the courage
    and the wisdom
    to let them be
        my teachers.

# Gifts

I looked at the circle of faces
    and asked a simple question.
     "What are your gifts?"
        And there was much coughing
        and clearing of throats,
        and shifting of seats,
        and silence.

Can it be, God,
    that you forgot to give this group
    any gifts at all?
Can it be, God, that you overlooked them,
    that they slipped through
    while skipping this step?

Or maybe it's not the gifts we're missing.
Maybe it's the eyes to see them.
    To see the gift
        in being able to bake a fresh coconut cake
        or to fix a phone
        as well as singing a solo.
    To see the gift
        in sending the perfect card
        or growing the flowers
        as well as teaching the class.

Maybe it's not the gifts we're missing,
    but the celebration of them.
        we don't want to brag on ourselves.
        We don't want to be proud.

God,
we'd be furious if a friend
received our gifts
the way we receive yours.
If they hid them away in a closet or drawer.
If they acted as if
the gift we'd been so careful to give
wasn't worth anything.
God, how do you feel
when we declare
we have no gifts to offer?

What do you think
when we declare
that what you've given us
with such great love
isn't really very good?

# Checking Our Bags

Where did we learn, God,
    to check our bags
    at the door of the church?

Where did we learn
    that we have to leave outside
    the heavy burdens of
        our questions
        and doubts
        and fears
        and hurts
            that stoop our shoulders
            and keep us awake at night.

Where did we learn
    that church is the place
    where we are always fine?

I didn't expect it, Lord,
    not even in a small group
    meant for such things.
        But right there
        in the midst of a church conference room
        we started telling the truth
        about our lives.
The truth about our struggles.
The truth about our hopes.
The truth about our faith.
    And I found myself speechless
    in the face of the grace
        that came like a cool breeze
        on a hot August night.
None of us were fine.
All of us were fine.

God,
      what would happen
      if we started
            telling the truth in church?
What if we asked the questions
      we'd always wanted to ask of scripture?
What if we didn't give
      the answers that were expected of us
      but the ones we really thought?
What would happen if we simply admitted to each other
      that sometimes we are anxious
      or worried
      or depressed.
That sometimes we fight
      with our spouses
      or with our children.
That as people of God
      we do not always know
      how to live the life of faith.

God,
      what would happen
      if we didn't check our bags at the door
            but brought them with us,
            sitting them beside us on a pew or in a chair.
We wouldn't even have to open them up.
Just bring them in
      so others would know
      we are not always fine.

Maybe . . .
      maybe grace would break out
      again.

# The Bad Kids

They're the bad kids.
>They know it.
>Everyone knows it.
>>They wear their reputations
>>like a proud tattoo.
Defiantly slouching.
Monosyllabic answers,
>and grunts
>and silences.
But peeking past the tough outsides,
>I see confusion
>and pain
>and fear.
Kids who've received
>blows instead of hugs.
Kids shuffled from one place to the next
>like hand-me-down furniture.
Kids who've never cared about anything
>because no on has ever
>cared about them.

God,
>why are we so quick
>to write people off?
Why are we so content
>to stand back in judgment?
>>Maybe because it's easier.
>>Maybe because we won't
>>>have our patience tried
>>>and our hearts broken.

Maybe because
   we don't like to play
   when the odds are so great
   and the stakes are so high.
         And so we write them off.
         They're the bad kids.

If only, God,
   if only we could see them
   through your eyes . . .

# My Heart Breaks for Her

My heart breaks for her.
I want to fix it,
        to make it all better,
But my useless hands
        hang heavy
        by my side.

I want to fix it, Lord,
        for I suffer to see her pain.
In the silence between us
        her agony slips over to my heart,
        tapping on it,
        leaving the smallest of reminders
        of her heartache.

I want to fix it, Lord,
        but I can't,
        and embarrassed by my failure,
        I want to avoid her.
                Not because I don't care, you see.
                Because I care so much
                        it frightens me,
                        it angers me
                        to be able to do so little.

God,
I can't make her pain go away.
But maybe,
        maybe you could help me
        to have the courage
        not to turn away from it,
Not to turn away from her.

Help me to offer
        what comfort is mine to offer,
        what comfort is yours to offer
                        through me.
Help us to remember
        that she is not alone . . .
        and neither am I.

# "Will Work for Food"

"Will work for food."
I see the sign and turn away,
    grateful for my sunglasses
    that keep him from catching my eyes.
He stands on the corner
    crowded with shoppers.

"He's smart,"
    I think to myself,
    "standing outside a mall,
    catching us while we're feeling guilty
    for having spent the money that we do have
        on what we really don't need."
And I am angry at his cleverness.

I stare straight ahead,
    praying for the light to change,
    reminding myself of all the news reports,
        the con artists among the beggars,
        the tax-free income,
        those who refuse the job offers that come.
And maybe, Lord,
    he's one of them.
That's what I tell myself
    when I drive away.
        But somehow I cannot leave behind
        the knowledge that some are truly hungry.
I cannot forget
    that some are working as hard as they know how,
    wrapping their arms around every single chance
        they get,
    and still the money runs out,

and the clothes wear clean through,
and the cupboard grows bare.
Forgive me, Lord,
when cynicism crowds out compassion.
Forgive me
when I choose to see
only those who are manipulating the system,
and not those who are crushed by it.
Forgive me
when I use another person's sinfulness and
brokenness
as an excuse not to hear your call
to feed the hungry
and clothe the naked.

Teach me, O Lord, how to do it.
Teach me how to be
as wise as a serpent and as innocent as a dove.
Let not the call of the con artist
shut my heart to the cries of the suffering.
Teach me to see, Lord.
Teach me to see clearly.

# Children

Her eyes grew somber,
and I could see
the sadness
in her five-year-old face,

It's so easy to overlook a child,
for we only see
that they have no bills to pay,
that they have vacations
that last all summer long,
that they get to take naps
without feeling guilty,
and we envy them.

Sometimes I forget
how intimidating the world is
when all you see are knees,
the utter terror of the first day at school
in a room full of strangers,
the all-too real grief
when the goldfish dies
or the cat runs away
or your best friend moves
to Outer Mongolia
(or maybe it just seems that far).

Sometimes I forget, God,
how long a day can seem
when you've had so few of them.

Help me, God,
to see the real people
standing in front of me,
    tired or scared
    or filled with way too much energy
    and way too many questions.

Help me, God,
    to see them by heart.

# The Keepers of Our Histories

Their eyes have grown cloudy,
    their hair sparse and white,
    and because they don't get around much anymore,
I am tempted to breeze right past them.
    I have places to go,
        things to do.
But Lord,
    when I do stop,
    when I do listen,
    what wondrous stories I hear . . .
Simple games and swimming holes.
Two-week revivals and funeral home fans.
Old schoolhouses and old friends,
    and mommas and daddies long since gone.
As they talk,
    their eyes light up
        with the light of all who have ever loved them,
    their eyes grow tender
        with the memory of all who have ever left
            them.
Thank you, Lord,
    for the tellers of stories,
    for the keepers of our histories.

# What Do You Say to Them, Lord?

He's thirteen years old, Lord,
    big for his age,
    with a smile as sweet as the morning air,
    a face still gentle and innocent.
    And now he is dead.

I do not understand it, Lord,
I cannot understand it,
    the babies whose lifetimes can be held in a single
        hand,
    the kids whose lifetimes are cut short
        like a film broken in mid-reel
        and we'll never know how the story could have
           ended.
I don't understand it, Lord,
    the ones whose bodies are invaded by disease,
    the ones in the wrong place at the wrong time,
    the ones who lift their own hands against
          themselves
        to stop the hurting,
        or to flaunt their anger,
        or to end a confusion grown too deep.
I can decipher the causes,
    the cells gone haywire,
    the slick roads and drunk drivers,
    the depression and fear and misunderstandings,
        but it makes no sense to me.
What do you say to them, Lord?
What do you say when they come to you?
Do they ever get a chance

to make up for what they missed?
What do you say to them?

Standing by a sweet, silent boy,
I am mute,
    for there are no words.

Help me, Lord,
    to know how to fight against what ought not to be,
    to have the faith to keep asking questions
        and the grace to accept your peace
        that has known both suffering
            and resurrection.

# Breakfast with a Friend

Eggs and grits.
Coffee and toast.
    A shuffle of cafeteria trays.
    A breakfast with a friend.

The time is woven
    with such common stuff, Lord.
Yet somehow our words
    dance in the air between us
    weaving their own cloth
        of wonder,
        of mystery,
        of grace.

Common place and ordinary meal.
Simple friendship.
    Words of work and schedules and families.
    Words of hopes and dreams and questions.
    Words of dawn and words of darkness.

Thank you, Lord,
    for the gift,
        the soul-stirring,
        spirit-warming,
        ordinary, rare gift
of conversation with friends.

# The Church
# That Laughs Together

We were so silly tonight, God,
    taking a bit of foolishness
    and hamming it up for all it was worth,

The Wednesday evening program
    had no socially redeeming quality
    except for the laughter it produced.
What an amazing thing to see—
    a fellowship hall
    full of laughter.

Thank you, God,
    for a church
    that can laugh together.
        For deacons not too dignified
            to don a silly outfit.
        For leaders not too preoccupied with power
            to risk milking a laugh
            for all it's worth.
        For upstanding, respectable members
            willing to act like fools
            for an evening.

For in our clowning around
    is the serious business of trust.
We trust you to laugh with us,
    not at us.
We trust you enough
    to lay aside our roles
        and titles

and positions
for the lowly place of jester.
Even as laughter strengthens our bodies,
so it seems
that laughter
strengthens
the body of Christ.

Thank you, God,
for the gift of a church
that loves enough
to laugh together.

# Passionate People

With grace and gratitude
    she celebrates her gifts,
    even the gift of her living.
Her spirit and her heart
    are in themselves
    an invitation
        for my own spirit to grow beyond
        the small and narrow limits
            I put upon it.

God,
    give us more passionate people
        whose eyes shine with visions,   .
        whose hearts beat with dreams,
        who simply, quietly do
            what others say cannot be done.

God,
    give us more passionate people.
    While others nibble on life
    and declare that a small taste
    is a gracious plenty,
        they dare to feast.
    While others count it enough
        simply to get by,
        simply to mark off another day,
            they live fully,
                freely,
                gladly.

God,
     give us more passionate people
     for blessed are they,
          the peacemakers,
          the healers,
          the ones who dare
               to be alive.

## Packing Well

There's a fine art to packing for a trip, in know-ing what's necessary to have, what will get in the way, and what can be easily replaced if we decide we need it after all. Sometimes after we arrive we discover that what we thought was absolutely necessary is really quite useless in this new place, and the little something or other that we threw in at the last minute becomes the most important thing of all.

So sometimes it is in faith that what ought to have inspired us leaves us cold. It's in hearing the laughter of loved ones, in seeing the sunlight on the dew of the first real day of spring, in what is so easy to overlook that God comes and speaks and leaves our hearts strangely warmed.

# Yard Shoes

I slipped them on,
     and I smiled.
Yard shoes.
     Worn leather
          stained with grass and mud.
     Worn-down soles
          uneven and slick.
A shoe past its prime
     now shaped by countless hours
     of cutting,
          and digging,
               and chopping,
                    and planting,
                         and dreaming,
                              and hoping.
Thank you, Lord,
     for the common,
          comfortable things.
In a world that changes too fast,
     thank you for familiar things.
In a world full of complicated technology,
     thank you for simple things.

Thank you, God,
     for a beat-up,
     not-fit-for-wearing-in-public
     pair of yard shoes.
For they ground me in the rich earth.
They carry me
     to the soul-satisfying work
     of tending creation.

They remind me
    that my spirit needs
        the warmth of the sun,
        and the grace of the breeze,
        and the promise of planting.

Thank you, Lord,
    for the utter honesty
    of a worn-out pair of yard shoes,
For I slip them on . . .
    and my heart smiles.

# Home

I walked through the door
    I've walked through a thousand times before.
I'd only been gone an hour or two,
    but still I felt it in my bones . . .
        I was home.

Surrounded by the things I'd collected,
    the gifts I'd been given,
    even the colors I'd chosen,
    the gladness of it went all the way to my heart.

But how can I forget the homeless, God?
The ones we all know about
    but seldom let ourselves see,
        living in shelters
    or taking shelter in cardboard boxes,
        beneath bridges,
        in an alleyway.

God,
    others have shelter but no home . . .
The ones in a nursing home
    that can never be completely home,
    as if half a room
    was space enough
        for an entire life.

The ones whose houses
    are carefully coordinated,
    decorator designed,
    magnificently beautiful showplaces
        that still remain strangely empty,

for somewhere along the way
people misplaced their souls
and lost themselves
and have no power
to transform this exhibition
into a home.

The ones whose houses
are places of violence and fear,
where spirits are always in danger
of being snuffed out
and bodies are always in danger
of being broken.
The ones whose only hope
is in leaving home.

God,
even as I give thanks
for the gift
of coming home,
let me never forget
all for whom home
is only
memory and dream.

# *Laughter*

Laughter.
In the midst of such serious work,
    it came spilling out
    as the absurdity of a moment
        caught up with us
        and would not let us go.

Laughter.
Every word,
    even those begun with serious intent
    to call us back to the matter at hand,
    led to more giggles,
        as out of control
            as snowballs racing downhill,
        as lightly unpredictable
            as bubbles dancing in the air.
Grown-up, respectable people,
We laughed
    until we held our sides,
    and the tears came flowing,
    and our faces hurt
        from the force of it.

When we finally caught our breath,
    it was as if we had laid aside
    great and heavy coats,
        for our spirits were lighter,
        our souls renewed.

Thank you, Lord, for laughter.
Thank you for the way
    it gets inside our bones and rattles around,
    and shakes us loose from our pretensions.
Thank you for the way
    that it glitters in the midst of us
    like so many shiny pieces of crystal,
        catching the light.
Thank you for the sentences that dissolve into giggles,
    the tears that are nothing but sheer joy.
    Thank you, Lord, for laughter.

# *Work*

It's time to go to work,
    and I am delighted.
    I am excited.

You know the truth, God,
    that I'm not always like this,
    that sometimes I mutter and whine
        and drag myself to the task at hand,
    that sometimes everything I touch
        is sheer frustration.

But you also know
    the better truth, God,
    that I love my work.
        A chance to use my gifts.
        The demand that I pay attention to my life
            and continue to grow.
        The honor and privilege
            of sharing in the journey
            of so many.
        The invitation to be witness
            to holy ground
            taking shape.
I love my work, God.
But I also know
    that's not a chorus
    you hear sung very often.

For so many people,
    too many people,
    work is punishment and not privilege.

Too many people
    work in places that chip away at them,

eat away at them,
    bit by bit.

Places where they are just another tool,
    just another machine,
    just another piece of furniture.
        Places that demand.
        and diminish
        and belittle.
            Work that has no rhythm
            except all-out
            as hard as you can go
            as many hours as you have.

I know some people
    work at jobs
    that drain away their lives little by little
    until they awake one morning
    to find themselves empty.
Even good work's not good
    if it isn't your work,
    if you have to silence your heart
    and lay aside your self.
I know some people
    who know the calling of their hearts
    all too well
    but can't find the way there.
        The path is blocked,
        the road has far too many detours,
        everything is fogged in.
            It appears to them as if
            they can't get there from here.

It's time to go to work,
and I am delighted.
God, help me never
to take such a gift for granted.
God, help me never
to quit working for a world
where all the work of our hands
may be blessed,
and we may be blessed
in the doing of it.

# First Snowfall

The weather reporters are breathless,
    an unhealthy gleam in their eyes.
        A storm is on its way,
        promising the first snowfall of the season.
In this snow-starved place,
    grown-ups dash to grocery stores,
    and children clamor for school to close.

And then the snow comes,
    slowly covering the landscape,
    slowly shifting the busy pace of our lives,
        For a moment the neighborhood noise
        is reduced
        to crystal silence.
Ordinary objects assume magical forms.
Ordinary walls are broken down
    as neighbors rediscover neighbors
    stomping along a street
        or sliding a sled.

Before we remember
    the inconvenience of it all,
Before the plows come
    and the slush accumulates
    and dealing with the snow
        becomes just one more thing to do,
In those first, wonder-filled hours,
    our worlds are transformed,
    and it is sheer magic.

God, may our eyes never become so jaded
    and our hearts so old
    that we miss the wonder
        of first snowfall.

# Children's Books

Sitting in the middle of the aisle,
    I read to myself
    and laugh out loud.
        I'm reading children's books again.
Thank you, God,
    for gifted writers and artists
    who tell the truth in such surprising ways.
    (The truth that some things
        make for terrible, very bad days.
    The truth that forever is a long time,
        at least until dinner.
    The truth that life is a lot easier
        with a dependable teddy bear by your side.
    The truth that you ought not to let
        sheep drive your jeep
        nor a cat in a hat in your house.)

Thank you, God,
    for gifted writers and artists
    who haven't become so grown-up
    that they've lost the wondrous gift
        of being silly,
        of making even the most important of us
            forsake our stiff, upper lip
            for a smile.

Thank you, God,
    for children's books.
        For all they gave me once upon a time,
        for all they give me now.

# Nothing to Wear

I stand at my closet door
    shifting my weight from foot to foot,
    pulling out,
    putting back
        with great frowns and sighs.
        I have nothing to wear.

Yes, God,
I know I have a closet
    quite full of clothes.
    Clothes that even fit
        (technically, at least).
            And yet,
            they don't fit at all.

Maybe what doesn't fit
    isn't outside at all.
Maybe it's inside.
    Maybe what I keep carrying around
        that I've long since outgrown.
    Maybe it's that to which I cling
        even after its outlived its usefulness.
    Maybe it's the something in me that knows
        it's time to move on
        to a new stretch of the journey.
            Maybe even it's you.

God,
    help me get my signals straight.
Help me to sort through the message
    so that when my soul cries out for pilgrimage
    I don't respond
        by going to the mall.

# Candlelight

A couple of hundred people,
    they stand gentle
    in the warm, inviting glow
    of the candles they hold.

There is in the light a mystery,
    a magic,
    a reminder that our world
    isn't always as flat and predictable
        as we would believe

I look out over the faces and realize
    my soul is hungry
    for magic and mystery.
        For not dissecting everything
        but simply embracing some things,
            To know that some truths can be proven,
            but others must be sung.

To know
    that some things
    I do not,
        cannot know.

God,
in this world
    where we know so much
    and understand so little,
        help me live the mysteries.

# The Tract

It came in the mail, Lord,
    sent from who knows where.
A piece of paper with extravagant pictures of heaven
    and lurid pictures of hell,
    and a listing of who would qualify
        for which place.
The words seemed so angry
    and so vindictive,
    and so absolutely sure
        of where the dividing lines would be drawn.

My God,
    it made my heart hurt to read it.
    For there was nothing of love in its pages,
    nothing of grace in its words.
I felt condemnation, not compassion.
    So eager to write off
    so many people.

I know you make demands of us,
    I know you ask of us to give our very lives.
But I can't help but believe
    that you want us to come to you
    prodded by the gentle nudging of love,
Not propelled by fears of hell.
I can't help but believe
    that you want us to greet you
    like children welcoming a parent home,
    not cringing like a child
        who's been beaten and battered
        and desperately tries to be good
            just to keep from being hurt again.

Still, I've got to confess
that it's all too easy for me
to point fingers at them
for pointing fingers at others.
God, forgive me
when I become self-righteous
about the self-righteousness of others.
Forgive all of us
when we wound and hurt and condemn
in the name of you who came to heal and to
redeem.

# Leaves and Letting Go

Outside my window
    the trees are showing the signs of fall.
While the branches of my tulip poplar
    are bare and spindly,
    leaves already fallen and raked
    and gathered up from the street,
the oak tree is only beginning
    to slide from green to burgundy-brown.

The years have taught me
    that these leaves won't fall until spring.
They won't let go
    until the new leaves push their way out.
Not until they have to,
    hanging on through the winter winds
        dry,
        brittle,
        and dead.
No wonder I feel a certain kinship with that tree.

How many times have I done it, Lord,
    holding on to old habits,
    old opinions,
    old visions
        long after the life had gone out of them?
How many times
    have you had to push and shove me
    kicking and screaming to the place
        I'd always wanted to go anyway?

How many times have I refused to accept your gift
    of what could be
    because I could not open my hands and let go
    of what has been?
        I must look as ridiculous
        as that old oak in March,
            fiercely holding on to last year's leaves,
            dry,
            brittle,
            and dead.

Remind me again
    that for everything there is a season,
    even a season of letting go.

# *Dancing*

I dance around the room
    and feel the joy
    working its way up
        from the souls of my feet
        to my heart and my head.
I dance,
    for my whole body
    needs to laugh.

I run,
I walk,
    and my legs find a rhythm
    that echoes the beating of my heart,
    the rise and fall of my lungs.
I run,
I walk,
    and the rhythm of my steps
    carves a place for the thoughts of my mind,
    a place where they may be sorted and seen.

I stretch,
    and muscles gladly let loose
    of tight-fisted tension,
    and the lines of my face
        fall easy and soft,
    and my breath comes
        easy and deep.

I dance,
    I run,
        I walk,
            I stretch.

Where did we get the idea, God,
    that we could know you only in our heads?
Where did we decide
    that our bodies were only an afterthought,
    a bit of wrapping paper
        encasing what really mattered?
How did we conclude
    that we could bring them into the picture of faith
    only when they were sick or broken?
        When did we forget
            that David danced before the Ark,
            that the psalmists
                leapt and danced
                and walked long ways as pilgrims
                with every step a prayer?

I dance,
    I run,
        I walk,
            I stretch,
                I move.
Hear, O God,
    my body's prayer.

# For Simple Things

Today, Lord,
I sing a song of praise
    for simple things . . .
    the way the early morning sun sifts through the
leaves,
    a warm hug from a good friend,
    the first cup of coffee on a cold winter's morning,
    a song I know by heart
        and sing to myself,
    an unexpected letter,
    fireflies and crickets on a summer's night.

Nothing earth-shaking.
Nothing that hasn't happened
    a thousand times
    to hundreds of thousands of people.

But today, Lord,
    today I see through different eyes,
    today I see that each ordinary gift
        when held and savored
        and lifted to the light
        glitters like diamonds.
God, we are swimming in them!
So today I say
    thank you
    for such simple,
    wonderful,
    thick-as-snowdrift miracles.